Sandcastles and Cucumberships Last Forever

by Theta Burke

Delafield Press • P.O. Box 8084 • Ann Arbor, Michigan 48107

Copyright 1978 © Theta Burke
All rights reserved.

ISBN: 9-916872-06-8
Library of Congress Catalog Card Number: 78-74555
Printed in the United States of America

First Edition

A note for you—

When I wrote these poems I had certain pictures in my mind to go with them—BUT I CAN'T DRAW! So I'm leaving some space here and there in the book if you'd like to draw your own "imaginations".

What do you think about poetry? I think it's a very special way of seeing things—of using your imagination and understanding to say how you feel about something or a certain way you see it. It doesn't really have to rhyme—and it can be short, medium or long.

When I write poetry or read it, I don't think about rules. I just think about what I enjoy. I hope that's how you'll read this book.

And I would like to see a copy of some of the pictures you might draw for some of the poems. Send them to me at P.O. Box 335, Suttons Bay, Michigan 49682.

Theta Burke,

WHAT'S INSIDE

Childhood Never Is Done 9
The Invisible Tiger 10
George 12
At My Birdfeeder 14
Twilight Creatures 15
The Menacing Cloud 16
Abraham Canary 17
Friends Are Always Near 18
The Magic Elves 19
Kenny's Gerbil 21
The Forgotten Easter Bunny 22
What Christmas Is 24
Do You See? 25
The Puzzled Little Snake 26
I'm A Raindrop 29
He Took More Time 30
My Dog 31
A Special Christmas Bell 32
The Substitute Frog 33
Little Star 35
My Friend in the Sky 38
Frog by the Sink 39
A Tiny Miracle 43
Your Genie 44
How? 45
My Cucumber Ship 47

CHILDHOOD NEVER IS DONE

I know a man named Mr. Kyle
I think he forgot he was ever a child
He's always sad and never does smile
And that's not the way it is with a child.

A child will be merry or angry or sad
He's mostly good but sometimes bad
He loves and forgives as he learns how to live
With a heart full of love, he knows how to give.

When some get old, it's sad they forget
And think their childhood already is spent
But folks who love and folks who have fun
Know that childhood never is done.

THE INVISIBLE TIGER

Now, Homer was a little tiger
Who lived in a cricket cage
No, a cricket didn't live there
'Cause that's the place where Homer stayed.

He'd come and go whenever he pleased
And you didn't need to feed him
He grew on love which people gave
And only certain folks could see him.

And if he grew you'd wonder how
He could keep on living in a cricket cage
But remember he grew from the love he knew
And most of that he gave away.

So, he could stay the size he'd wish
To keep on living in his cage
And so long as people loved him
That's where Homer liked to stay.

GEORGE

I have a frog whose name is George
(Not "real" as some folks see)
He's made of cloth and soft insides
But he's very real to me.

He often comes along to play
And he sometimes stays at home
We talk about a lot of things
As he tells me things he knows.

He says he's glad to have me see
That he's important in a special way
'Cause some don't know — and miss a lot
About some things life has to say.

He says if folks just pay attention
To things they can touch and see
They can't know those special pleasures
That fantasies bring to George and me.

AT MY BIRDFEEDER

My hungry little chickadee
Hurries down to peck a seed
He looks around and darts away
I just hope he's not afraid.

I guess he has to learn my face
Before he feels that he is safe
And that may take a little while
For making friends can take some time.

TWILIGHT CREATURES

Wispy, shadowy, twilight creatures
When you're a little afraid of the dark
Appear for minute then go away
And you're left to wonder if they *are*.

You're not quite sure but you don't want to ask
'Cause folks might think you're silly
So you imagine all sorts of things
That drive you willy-nilly.

Just say to yourself as you think of the shadows
Perhaps they really can't see in the light
And ghostly shadows are friendly things
That can only come out at night.

Then the shadows and you will learn to be friends
When you're not afraid of each other
For the sun keeps the day and the moon keeps the night
And neither's afraid of the other.

THE MENACING CLOUD

I saw the approaching cloud
    swallow a star.
And the nearby moon
    moved as to rescue
    and was swallowed, too!

ABRAHAM CANARY

He begins his morning singing
In a muted kind of way
When all is quiet within the house
In the early part of day

When no one answers, he's still for a bit
His cover's on his cage
But pretty soon he tries again
To see if we're awake

How happy he is to say Good Morning
When the cover's lifted off
He shows his happiness in concert
Such a repertoire of song.

FRIENDS ARE ALWAYS NEAR

I have a friend who's going away
And I would like my friend to stay
But he will not forget, says he,
He will still remember me.

And memories make a friendship live
With the loving that we give
And though a friend be far away
Love can make the friendship stay.

THE MAGIC ELVES

Whenever a useful thought is born
A magic elf comes with it
To do whatever thing we'd ask
It's sad we so seldom use it.

Dreams and thoughts we cast aside
Never giving them leave to work
Magic elves with magic powers
With never a chance to do their work.

They're sad and lost when they're not used
They think you feel they're not worthwhile
How eager they are to please you
Please, oh, please don't push them aside.

If you'll only begin the action
All their magic they'll start to use
Happy, joyous, working elves
Doing what you want them to.

Millions and millions of sad, sad elves
Are neglected and cast aside
Wasted power and wasted good
Because their worth isn't recognized.

So anytime you have a dream
About a thing that you would do
Just know the elves are right there waiting
To do whatever you tell them to.

KENNY'S GERBIL

He had a little gerbil
To care for and to feed
He cleaned his cage and played with him
And learned the things which gerbils need.

He'd pick him up and hold him
Like he wished someone would do to him
And he didn't know how tight he held
But a bit too tight for the gerbil to live.

And when he knew what he had done
It made him very sad
But he learned that holding on too tightly
Had caused the loss of what he had.

THE FORGOTTEN EASTER BUNNY

A chocolate Easter bunny
Sat all alone on a shelf
He felt a chocolate tear melt down
Because it seemed that he'd been left.

He looked around for the Easter eggs
That had waited there with him
He'd thought they'd leave together
But they were gone — they'd forgotten him.

He wondered what he'd ever do
With no one to make glad
He felt another tear melt down
A chocolate bunny feeling sad.

But then he heard a door unlatch
And saw a tiny boy
Who came toward him — eyes all bright
Reflecting Easter joy.

Happy they were to find each other
Each made the other glad
And as the boy took him from the shelf
The Easter Bunny no longer felt sad.

WHAT CHRISTMAS IS

Don't let Christmas ever be
A day that's just another day
Take some time to think about
The special things it has to say.

Don't just focus on the Christmas tree
Or the gifts that rest below
Remember the reason behind it all
And share the love you've learned to know.

For Christmas is a day of celebration
Of that special feeling we know as love
And the joy we feel in sharing this
Makes us *know* that God is Love.

DO YOU SEE?

I blundered into a spider's web
I said I'm sorry — I did not see
What beauty you were building
Would you please forgive me.

The spider was very pleasant
He said, I'll build another
I have lots of spinning thread
And it really is no bother.

But, said he, I thank you
For stopping to say you care
Most folks wouldn't even know
Hardly anyone sees what's here.

THE PUZZLED LITTLE SNAKE

There was once a little snake
Who was playing in the grass
He was having fun with the other snakes
And then some people passed

They looked at him and ran in fright
And this surprised him so!
He thought there was something wrong with him
And he'd really like to know

So he asked his friends — some other snakes
Who pondered with him the question
But none came up with an answer
Not even a slight suggestion

He talked it over with other friends
Who also lived in the woods
They all felt sad for the little snake
And said they'd do whatever they could

Now after a while the wise old owl
Thought perhaps he had a clue
So he had a conference with the little snake
To discuss what he should do

He said — Now I have noticed that when you walk
    you wiggle around
And go in lots of funny ways
So maybe you have to try to find
How to walk in a straighter way

So the little snake gave this some thought
And he said it might be so
So he'd practice some till he could see
If straight he could really go

It surely did seem awkward
Walking just wasn't right that way
And how would he ever have any fun
If he tried to be the people's way

He decided that people must be afraid
Of things they didn't understand
But he'd have to be just the way he was
'Cause that's what Mother Nature planned.

I'M A RAINDROP

I'm a tiny drop of water
That's going to the sea
And though I'm very little
I think the sea has need of me.

For if each of us thought he didn't matter
How dry the sea would be
So if ever you feel you're not important
Just remember that raindrops make the sea.

HE TOOK MORE TIME

He was a little behind the rest of the flock
On his Northward journey home
He'd lingered sometimes along the way
For a bit of time alone.

The others didn't always understand
They thought he tried to delay
Their goal was to reach their home ahead
He savored the pleasures along the way.

So it took him a little longer
To arrive at the appointed place
But he came a fuller and wiser bird
He knew it was a journey
      and not a race.

MY DOG

Taffy is my special friend
Who hears the way I feel
I may put on a front to others
She always knows just what is real

She may not know just what to do
Whenever she sees me cry
But she sits right close beside me
And never questions why

With Taffy I can be what's me
I know she loves me for myself
No admonition does she give
That I should be a better self

So very rare is such a friend
Who takes us as we are
Who knows that just from loving
We learn the freedom of who we are.

A SPECIAL CHRISTMAS BELL

A tiny little Christmas bell
Made of beads and thread
Hung upon the Christmas tree
And this is what it said:

I'm a bell 'cause someone dreamed me
I used to be some different things
But she saw a way that beads and thread
Could make a bell — I just can't ring.

But that's okay — I'm awfully proud
To be a bell upon the tree
And I'm glad somebody saw a way
To make a Christmas bell like me.

THE SUBSTITUTE FROG

I'm not the brown frog that you ordered
But I may be more than I might seem
And I hope you're not disappointed
'Cause I'm just an ordinary green.

Because somebody chose my cloth
That came in a different color
I hope you'll wait to get to know me
Before you decide you don't like my color.

We frogs have a lot of different ways
To speak the things inside
And that's the part that really matters
And if you look, that's what you'll find.

I know lots of different frogs
That come in many different colors
But our inside parts are a lot the same
Because, you see, we're brothers.

So I shall come to live with you
'Til the Maker of Frogs finds your special color
And we might just get to like each other
And then I'd live with you forever.

LITTLE STAR

Hi, Little Star
You're awfully pretty
Way up there.

You're really not little
But that's what they say
You just look like that
    'cause you're far away!

SNOW MAGIC

There was something about the snow
While he was yet a little boy
Something about the watching it fall
That filled his heart with joy.

And when he'd heard that it might snow
Early tomorrow morn
Before he went to bed he'd set
His tiny little alarm.

He'd get up quietly while dark it was
And tiptoe to the window
To wait for the magic flakes to fall
That filled his head with wonder.

At first they'd flutter slowly down
Then start to gain momentum
And he'd watch the whiteness cover his world
Such a magic picture from his window.

MY FRIEND IN THE SKY

The moon is my friend who lives in the sky
He sees the reasons and he knows the why's
He watches what happens on land or on sea
And what I need know, he tells it to me.

I love my moon in all its shapes
As it speaks its message to me
It's a longtime friend from childhood
Who shares the spirit of night with me.

And no matter how or where I am
Its presence speaks a peaceful quiet
And I feel glad whenever I see
My silent sentinel of the night.

FROG BY THE SINK

Little Frog sits
By the kitchen sink
And every day
He thinks and thinks
And if he gets thirsty
He takes him a drink

'Cause somebody always
Is splashing some water
Though they really don't know
He has need of the water

They think he is only
Made of clay
But he doesn't mind
It's really okay

Someday somebody
Will come along
Who really will know
That he's more than a frog.

Now one sunny day
Who should come by
But a tousled haired boy
Who stopped and said - Hi
You're not really a frog, said he
You're probably a prince in disguise.

The frog sat right still
Hardly containing his joy
To hear that his secret
Was known by the boy.

For his special mission
Was that others would see
Beyond the things
That might seem to be.

A TINY MIRACLE

A leaf did break
From my little plant
And I wondered if it hurt
So I picked it up
And planted it
In a little bit of dirt.

It said its thanks by growing
And putting out new leaves
A tiny little miracle
That helped me bigger ones to see.

YOUR GENIE

A tiny twinkle I saw in a lamp
Before the lamp was lit
It came — and quickly disappeared
And I wondered where it went.

Some tiny fairy I thought perhaps
Just might be flitting about
To see what made the light turn bright
While still the light was out.

For a light is like a bit of magic
That comes when you turn a switch
Just like the genie of long ago
Who'd do whatever you'd wish.

And we each have our special genie
Who's at our beck and call
If we really do believe he's there
He'll answer when we call.

He's a mixture of hope and work and faith
That causes whatever thing to be
That we would like our lives to show
And love's the light that makes us see.

HOW?

The young child asked his mother
"How can I know God?
I've never even seen him
Or ever heard him talk."

His mother thought for a little bit
To see how she'd explain
A truth so great and yet so simple
That God was love by another name.

So she told him a little story
That his years could understand
That the ways we show our love to God
Are the ways we love our fellow man.

MY CUCUMBER SHIP

I went to the pond down by the barn
To launch my little ship
Made of a cucumber all scooped out
With a paper sail that tipped.

Ah - the adventures that we had
As we sailed upon our sea
The fact that it was only a little pond
Didn't matter to my ship and me.

For we were dreaming of future days
When we'd sail a bigger sea
And we knew whatever things we'd dream
Those things could really be.